BEST SHOTS

THE GREATEST PHOTOGRAPHY IN NASCAR HISTORY

BEST SHOTS

THE GREATEST PHOTOGRAPHY
IN NASCAR HISTORY

FOREWORD BY RICHARD PETTY

DK PUBLISHING

⫻NASCAR BEST SHOTS

LONDON, NEW YORK, MUNICH,
MELBOURNE, AND DELHI

04 05 06 07 08 09 10 9 8 7 6 5 4 3 2 1

Published in the United States in 2004 by DK Publishing, Inc.
375 Hudson Street, New York, New York 10014

Nascar is a registered trademark of the National Association for
Stock Car Auto Racing, Inc.

A catalog record for this book is available from the Library of Congress

DK Publishing, Inc.:
Project Editor: Anja Schmidt
Designer: Tai Blanche
Senior Designer: Michelle Baxter
DTP: Milos Orlovic
Production Manager: Chris Avgherinos
Art Director: Dirk Kaufman
Project Director: Sharon Lucas
Creative Director: Tina Vaughan
Publisher: Chuck Lang

NASCAR Publishing:
Senior Manager of Publishing: Jennifer White
Account Executive: Ashley Costello

Produced by:
SHORELINE PUBLISHING GROUP LLC
Santa Barbara, California
President/Editorial Director: James Buckley, Jr.
Designer: Thomas Carling, Carling Design Inc.

Color reproduction by ColourScan, Singapore
Printed and bound by Donnelly, USA

PHOTOGRAPHY CREDITS:

AP/Wide World 20, 38, 39, 44, 55, 56, 58, 146, 147
AP/Wide World photographers: John Basemore 156; David Boe 26;
Rusty Burroughs 86; Chuck Burton 11; Stephen J. Carrera 87;
Paul Connors 160; Peter Cosgrove 10; Roy Dabner 90; Bill Elliott 31;
Ric Field 77; Jon Fletcher/Florida Times-Union 18; Chris Gardner 6,
102, 143; David Graham 108; Tony Gutierrez 145, 150;
Julie Jacobson 91; Eric Jamison 131; Bob Jordan 152;
Wilfredo Lee 134; Will Lester 13; Doug McSchooler 126;
Steve Mitchell 151; Pablo Martinez Mosivais 34; Ken Newberry 43;
Sue Ogrocki 109; Chris O'Meara 135; Wade Payne 25; Erik Perel 153;
Emily Reily 24; Roger Simms/Daytona Beach News-Journal 54;
Greg Suvino 30; Jim Tiller: 136.

Brian Bahr/Allsport/Getty Images 64; John Chiasson/Getty Images:
138; Brian Cleary/Getty Images 9 bottom;

Brian Cleary/ISC 7, 8, 23, 48, 73, 78, 94, 98, 122, 139, 157;
CIA Stock Photo Inc. 2, 50, 57, 59, 76, 104, 105, 112, 127, 130,
133, 137, 139, 140, 142; Cy Jaris Cyr/Corbis 66;
Craig Jones/Allsport/Getty Images 69; ISC Archives 21, 82, 92, 106,
120, 121; Sheryl Creekmore/NASCAR 9 top, 22, 42, 51, 62, 63, 65,
68, 80, 81, 96, 97, 113, 116, 117, 124; Jon Ferrey/Allsport/Getty
Images 52, 72, 88, 103; Michael Kim/Corbis; Robert Laberge/Getty
Images 17; David Madison/NewSport/Corbis 118;
Al Messerschmidt 36, 37; David Miralle/Getty Images 128;
William Sallaz/Corbis 110; Sam Sharpe/Corbis 28, 125, 132;
Jeff Siner/Corbis 101; Brian Spurlock/Sports Gallery 45;
Jamie Squire/Getty Images 35, 40, 70, 74; Chris Stanford/Getty
Images 154; David Taylor/Allsport/Getty Images 60, 100, 144;
George Tiedemann 5, 14, 16, 19, 27, 32, 46, 84, 114, 115, 148, 158;
George Tiedemann/Corbis; 12; Kevin Wakefield/ISC 83, 93.

COMIN' AT YA!

PAGE 1:
RICKY RUDD ROARS INTO VIEW,
LEADING OFF *BEST SHOTS* WITH THIS
HEAD-ON VIEW FROM 2000.

LINED UP AND READY

PAGES 2-3:
THE FIELD IS READY ON PIT ROW
BEFORE THE START OF THE 2003
TROPICANA 400 AT HOMESTEAD-MIAMI
SPEEDWAY IN FLORIDA.

COLORFUL CHAOS

OPPOSITE:
BEFORE A RACE, THE GARAGE AND PIT
AREAS OF NASCAR TRACKS ARE AWASH
IN COLOR AS CREWS WORK FEVERISHLY
TO PREPARE THEIR CARS FOR THE HARD
WORK AHEAD. HERE THEY'RE READYING
THE VEHICLES BEFORE A 1999 RACE
AT MARTINSVILLE SPEEDWAY
IN MARTINSVILLE, VIRGINIA.

MESSAGE FROM "THE KING"

BY RICHARD PETTY

I've only missed watching about a dozen NASCAR races since the circuit started in 1949. If I wasn't taking part in the history, I was watching it. That's a lot of great memories. This book helps me think back on quite a few of those memories.

As you look through the book like I did, you'll look at some of the pictures just as pictures. Others you'll associate with a memory or a feeling. You see Matt Kenseth's crew on the wall (page 153), waiting for their driver to cross the finish line in first place, and you just feel what they're anticipating. I think our fans will take a lot of those feelings away from this book.

Things sure have changed over the years, though. All you have to do is look at the pictures of cars running on the beach (page 82) and then at the many pictures from today's cars running on a superspeedway. The tracks are different, the cars sure are different! Everything has changed in NASCAR, but that's true all over the world.

As far as the racin'—well, racin's racin'. It's been good no matter what the era.

Looking at that photo of my dad, my brother Maurice, and me (page 58) takes me back to the beginning. When we first started it was strictly stock. Got the cars straight off the showroom floor. Took off the muffler, put in a seatbelt, and that was it. Today, they look stock, but they're race cars built from the chassis up.

The driver's role has changed, too. He has become more a part of a team than a solo operator. That's the key to racing today, having a great team. You'll see a lot of teamwork in action in this book.

Several pictures in particular got me thinking: The book starts off with a lot of patriotic photos. After the terrible events of September 11, 2001, our people really got behind that feeling for our country. I like that part of the book and of our NASCAR scene.

I'm sitting in a Blue Angels cockpit on page 18. That was a real treat. We grew up in a little place out here in the [North Carolina] country, yet because of racing, I've been to the White House, been to Australia, England, all around the world. But that jet ride was a whole new trip. I'm used to speed, but we were pulling more than 6 Gs up there. For about 45 minutes, that pilot was trying to scare me and he did a good job!

Check out the close finish at Darlington in 2003 (page 122). Our team wasn't involved, but I got excited watching it! Seeing that photo takes me back to some close finishes in my own career. I remember in my last win [the 1984 Firecracker 400], Cale Yarborough and I were banging sides just like those guys at Darlington.

There are several great shots of pit crews in action. In the old days, pit stops were chaos. We've gone from bumper jacks to hyrdraulic jacks, and lug wrenches to air guns.

I liked seeing the photos of the different tracks in this book. People ask me what my favorite track was and I always tell them that anyplace I won—I loved! I was so engrossed in racing, if they called it a racetrack, I was happy. I just loved driving no matter where it was. When I look at these pictures, I can understand all of them, because I've been there and done that. If you show me a picture of a car on a race track I can pretty much tell you what track it is. I've been around those places so much that I understand the tracks more than I even realize.

However, I guess we Pettys have a special feeling for Daytona, and there are several great shots of that famous track in this book. My dad won the first 500 in 1959 and then my team was lucky enough to win seven of them. As Daytona grew in importance, I was fortunate enough to be in my prime. Daytona, NASCAR, and I grew up together—there's a bunch of history here!

The book also has several great shots of drivers and teams celebrating, often in Victory Lane. Let me tell you, reaching that is the ultimate feeling. What you did all week or all day leads up to that crowning moment. You had a goal and you reached it.

For me, though, it was about more than winning. It was all about self-satisfaction. There were nights after I won races that I didn't sleep because I wasn't happy with how I'd run. Then there were

races I ran fifth or sixth and slept fine knowing that I had done the best I could do that day. A lot of it for me comes down to not what others see, but what you feel about yourself and your effort.

Finally, you'll also see several great photos of fans enjoying NASCAR action. I've always appreciated the support of many people over my career. You gotta figure that no matter what we do, it's a fan's sport. It's their support that makes it work. It comes down to the people who buy the tickets and follow racing. They make it possible for us to do what we love to do. Whenever I meet a fan looking for an autograph or a photo, I think, "Thanks for letting us do what we love."

This book is a great effort to say thanks to the fans again and to capture some of the feelings and events, people and places of NASCAR. I hope you enjoy the ride!

PETTY ROARS TOWARDS THE FINISH LINE IN ONE OF HIS FINAL RACES IN 1992.

Richard "The King" Petty is the all-time winningest driver in NASCAR history, with 200 career wins. He also won seven NASCAR season championships, seven Daytona 500s, and more honors than you could fit in an eighteen-wheeler. After retiring from driving in 1992, he was awarded the Presidential Medal of Freedom, America's highest civilian award, for his work on and off the track. Today, as head of

Petty Enterprises, he leads a team of crew and drivers on the track. Off the track, Petty has long been involved with helping others. One of the efforts to which he lends great support is the Victory Junction Gang Camp in North Carolina, which annually treats hundreds of children battling chronic and life-threatening illnesses to a summer of camping fun. Learn more about it at www.victoryjunction.org.

LIGHTNING-FAST SHOOTING

You think NASCAR's cars are fast? You should see NASCAR photographers in action. And you can see them—or at least the results of their own lightning-fast action—in this photograph-filled book, which includes more than 110 of the greatest, coolest, wildest, fastest, most beautiful images from the NASCAR scene. These spectacular photographs represent the work of dozens of photographers from most of the NASCAR races that take place on tracks around the country.

Photographers covering NASCAR face challenges far different from other sports. For instance, a baseball photog-

BRIAN CLEARY SHOT THIS THREE-WIDE ACTION AT THE 2003 DAYTONA 500.

rapher typically stays in one place for most of a game. A football photographer only has to cover 100 yards at the most, a basketball shooter even less. And the action they're shooting, while very fast indeed, is nothing compared to the speed of NASCAR. At each track, NASCAR photographers are faced with capturing vehicles moving nearly 200 miles per hour on racing facilities covering several square miles!

"I once calculated that a car moving 200 miles per hour moves about seven feet in the fraction of a second that my shutter clicks," says veteran photographer George Tiedemann. "They cover an entire football field in about a second. Capturing that motion takes a lot of good timing and experience."

"You can pan [move the camera in synch] with them if you practice it," adds photographer Brian Cleary, a longtime regular on the NASCAR circuit. "I zero in on a number on the car and keep it centered in my viewfinder as I move the camera. That can compensate for the speed in most cases."

What comes out of the camera when wielded by expert shooters can be stunning, a frozen visual of high speed. From the action-blurred photograph on page 16 and a painterly palette of color on page 27, to the high, wide, and handsome, banked-track photo on page 72, the action on the tracks makes for some spectacular images.

Along with sharp eyes and technical expertise, photographers need stamina to get around the racing facilities during a race.

"Knowing the tracks is the key to success," says Tiedemann. "I usually shoot the start of a race from the infield, then drive out [through the tunnel beneath most tracks] with my gear and spend the next part of the race shooting from the grandstand. As the race nears the end, I drive back in to get the finish and then Victory Lane." Tiedemann also notes that at some racing facilities, he might have to walk a mile or more carrying all of his heavy camera gear.

Brian Cleary follows a similar plan, and his day sounds as organized as a driver's. "I try to start outside the track and work my way to the inside. I cover the start outside at Turn 1, stay there about 20 to 30 laps. Then I move up to the press box to shoot high. Back to the infield side, I head to the pits, shooting [he means photographing, of course] fans on the way. Then it's time for capturing the victory and then Victory Lane. Mapping it out ahead of time works best."

NASCAR is more than just roaring cars and huge tracks, however. Roaring crowds play a part, and in these pages you'll meet some of the thousands of fans who pack tracks around the country each weekend.

Going behind the scenes at racing facilities with a camera helps photographers provide those fans unadulterated views of their heroes, their cars, and their crews, that they couldn't find anywhere else.

Sheryl Creekmore has been covering NASCAR for five years, most recently as part of NASCAR's official coverage. "I prefer the human interaction of photography. You can get to know someone in a new way through the camera."

Tiedemann concurs. "The characters and personalities of the drivers is what makes NASCAR special. Also, you get access to them that you can't get in other sports."

Along with an eye for faces (page 22), Creekmore also has an eye for color and different angles on familiar subjects. On pages 116-117, she turns groups of trucks and cars into a kind of art.

Exciting races, fast cars, awesome tracks, engaging and emotional people, photographic art, and raw talent . . . it's a winning combination and all the ingredients fill this book. Turn the page and catch the action.

The photo on pages 122-123 shows how Cleary combined skill, timing, and, he admits, a little luck. He perfectly captured the exact millisecond that showed the closest finish in NASCAR history at Darlington in 2003.

"I normally use a camera that shoots eight frames a second, but it was broken. I could only shoot three frames per second with the camera I was using, so when they came out of Turn 4 neck-and-neck, I just held down the shutter and I got lucky. When I looked at the pictures I saw I got them right on the line."

Good planning can also make history. On page 84, you can experience a unique photo of the poignant moment when Dale Earnhardt Sr. and Jr. started a race together for the final time. Tiedemann created that photograph by activating a remote camera that he admits he almost didn't set up. NASCAR fans can be glad he did.

Photographers definitely see tracks in a different way than the rest of us. Tiedemann enjoys the dusky light at Lowe's Motor Speedway in North Carolina for the evening Coca-Cola 600 race, while Cleary likes shooting at Watkins Glen in upstate New York for the unique angles and points of view that road course offers.

PATRIOTIC PAUSE

A COLORFUL ARRAY OF PIT CREW MEMBERS LINE UP
IN THE TRADITIONAL PRE-RACE FORMATION AS THE
NATIONAL ANTHEM IS SUNG AT THE DAYTONA
INTERNATONAL SPEEDWAY IN DAYTONA BEACH,
FLORIDA, FOR THE 2003 PEPSI 400.

CALM BEFORE THE STORM

THE PACE CAR IS IN PLACE, THE OFFICIALS ARE
STANDING BY, THE DRIVERS ARE IN THEIR SEATS...
IT'S JUST ABOUT TIME TO RACE AT THE 2003 SHARPIE
500 AT BRISTOL MOTOR SPEEDWAY
IN BRISTOL, TENNESSEE.

RED, WHITE, BLUE, AND ORANGE

AMID THE HUSTLE AND BUSTLE OF PRE-RACE
PREPARATIONS, CREWS TAKES A BREAK BEFORE THE
2003 COCA-COLA 600 AT LOWE'S MOTOR SPEEDWAY
IN CONCORD, NORTH CAROLINA.
CASEY MEARS' PIT CREW JOIN THE CROWD IN
HONORING THE MEMORIAL DAY HOLIDAY.

A REAL AIRBORNE FLAG

MEMBERS OF THE 101ST AIRBORNE HOIST OLD
GLORY ALOFT PRIOR TO THE 2003 AUTO CLUB 500
AT CALIFORNIA SPEEDWAY IN FONTANA, CALIFORNIA.
A PRE-RACE SALUTE TO AMERICA IS PART OF EVERY
NASCAR EVENT.

FANS' EYE VIEW
PREVIOUS SPREAD:
THE PACKED SEATS AT MARTINSVILLE SURROUND THE
ACTION ON THE TRACK AND THE CROWDED AND
BUSTLING INFIELD IN THIS "END ZONE" VIEW.

HOW HE GOT THERE
MATT KENSETH ENSURED HIS 2003 NASCAR
CHAMPIONSHIP WITH SURE AND STEADY SUCCESS.
CONSISTENCY, INCLUDING 27 TOP 10 FINISHES,
WAS THE KEY TO VICTORY.

TOP OF THE WORLD

MATT KENSETH EXULTS ATOP THE ULTIMATE VICTORY
STAND, PREPARING TO HOIST THE 2003 NASCAR
WINSTON CUP SERIES CHAMPIONSHIP TROPHY.
HE HAS JUST FINISHED ADDING HIS NAME TO THE
ARRAY OF PAST CHAMPIONS SPELLED OUT ON THE
FLAGS BEHIND HIM.

KING OF THE SKIES

NASCAR LEGEND RICHARD PETTY (ABOVE) IS USED
TO GOING FAST. BUT IN 2003, HE GOT A NEW TASTE
OF SPEED WHEN HE TOOK A RIDE WITH THE
U.S. AIR FORCE'S FAMOUS BLUE ANGELS.

LOOK, UP IN THE SKY!

A FLIGHT OF U.S. AIR FORCE F-15S ROAR OVER A
THRILLED CROWD BEFORE THE 2003 COCA-COLA 600
AT LOWE'S MOTOR SPEEDWAY (RIGHT).

DANG, THAT'S FAST!
NASCAR LEGEND FIREBALL ROBERTS (RIGHT) LOOKS
ON AS CREW CHIEF "BANJO" MATTHEWS DISPLAYS
THE RECORD QUALIFYING SPEED ROBERTS
PUT UP BEFORE THE 1962 WORLD 600 AT
CHARLOTTE, NORTH CAROLINA.

CARRYOVER SUCCESS

JIM PASCHAL WAS ONE OF A NUMBER OF DRIVERS
WHO ENJOYED SUCCESS FIRST ON THE DIRT TRACKS
OF THE 1950S AND THEN ON THE ASPHALT
SPEEDWAYS OF THE 1960S. PASCAL RACKED UP
25 CAREER NASCAR RACE VICTORIES.

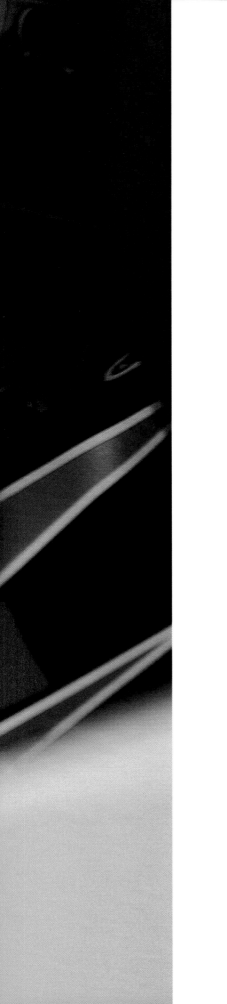

EYING THE PRIZE
A GOOD-LUCK KISS FROM HIS MOTHER
STILL WARM ON HIS CHEEK, NASCAR
BUSCH SERIES DRIVER SHANE HMIEL
(LEFT) AWAITS THE WORD TO CRANK UP
HIS ENGINE FOR THE 2003 MBNA ARMED
FORCES FAMILY 200 AT DOVER
INTERNATONAL SPEEDWAY IN
DOVER, DELAWARE.

GO!
THE OFFICIAL STARTER AT THE 2003
TROPICANA 400 AT HOMESTEAD-MIAMI
WAVES THE GREEN FLAG THAT SETS
THE FIELD A-RACIN' (ABOVE). STARTERS
ARE STATIONED ABOVE THE TRACK
THROUGHOUT THE RACE TO SIGNAL
DRIVERS WITH FLAGS.

SMOKE GETS IN THEIR RIDES
NASCAR BUSCH SERIES DRIVER BRAD LEIGHTON
SPREADS SMOKE ON PURPOSE AFTER WINNING A 2003
RACE AT NEW HAMPSHIRE INTERNATIONAL SPEEDWAY
AT LOUDON, NEW HAMPSHIRE (ABOVE).
IN A DIFFERENT NASCAR BUSCH SERIES RACE THAT
YEAR (RIGHT), DAVID GREEN SENDS OUT SMOKE
SIGNALS OF A DIFFERENT SORT AS HE HEADS THE
WRONG WAY DOWN THE TRACK!

BUMP 'N' RUN
NASCAR DRIVERS KNOW THAT A LITTLE (LEGAL)
PUSHING AND SHOVING CAN SOMETIMES BE THE PATH
TO THE FRONT OF THE PACK, AS SHOWN BY
JOHN ANDRETTI AND TONY RAINES AT THE
2003 SYLVANIA 300 AT NEW HAMPSHIRE.

BOXED IN

AND YOU THINK YOUR DRIVE TO WORK IS TOUGH:
JEFF GORDON (24) FINDS HIMSELF BOXED IN BY
SEVERAL RACERS DURING THE FIRST OF THE
TWIN 125S QUALIFYING RACES HELD PRIOR TO THE
2003 DAYTONA 500.

BROTHERLY LOVE

TERRY LABONTE (5) LEADS BROTHER BOBBY (18) AND
JEFF GORDON (24) DURING THE 2003 RUNNING OF
THE CHEVY ROCK & ROLL 400 AT RICHMOND
INTERNATIONAL RACEWAY IN RICHMOND, VIRGINIA.

TOW TRUCK TIME

NOT EVERY TIME OUT ON THE TRACK IS A DRIVE IN THE PARK. AT THIS 1990 NASCAR BUSCH SERIES RACE, NEARLY HALF OF THE FIELD WAS INVOLVED IN THIS TANGLE-UP, BUT NO ONE WAS SERIOUSLY INJURED . . . EXCEPT THE CARS, THAT IS.

AND ONE CAME THROUGH

Brian Vickers (5) races away from trouble during the 2003 Aaron's 312 NASCAR Busch Series race at Talladega Superspeedway in Talladega, Alabama in 2003. Brian escaped this 20-car fender-bender to continue the race.

A ROARING START
PREVIOUS SPREAD:
FANS AT LOWE'S MOTOR SPEEDWAY
CHEER AS THE FIELD TAKES OFF AT THE
START OF THE 2003 COCA-COLA 600,
EVENTUALLY WON BY JIMMIE JOHNSON,
WHO STARTED NEAR THE BACK
OF THE PACK.

DRIVER IN CHIEF
PRESIDENT GEORGE W. BUSH (ABOVE)
LOOKS LIKE HE'S JUST PARKED HIS
RIDE IN FRONT OF THE WHITE HOUSE.
ACTUALLY, HE WAS JUST CHECKING
OUT THE CARS ON HAND FOR HIS
MEETING WITH 2003 NASCAR WINSTON
CUP SERIES CHAMP MATT KENSETH.

FAST-MOVING FLAG
THE STANDS AT DAYTONA FORM A RED,
WHITE, AND BLUE BACKDROP FOR
AN EQUALLY PATRIOTICALLY COLORED
DALE JARRETT AS HE RACES
IN QUALIFYING FOR THE
1999 DAYTONA 500 (RIGHT).

NEXT GENERATION
AS A RACER, DALE EARNHARDT JR. (NO. 8 AT RIGHT)
FOLLOWS IN THE TIRE TREADS OF HIS LEGENDARY
FATHER. BUT IN THIS 2000 RUNNING OF THE
WINSTON AT LOWE'S MOTOR SPEEDWAY, IT WAS
DALE JR. WHO WAS LEADING THE WAY OVER
HIS POP IN THE NO. 3 CAR.

BEFORE THE COWBOY HAT
The career of Richard Petty, which began in
the late 1950s (above) and continued through
the peak of his success in the 1960s and 1970s
(left), traces the rise of NASCAR in the
American sports world.

BLUE SKY . . . THREE WIDE

FLUFFY CLOUDS IN A STUNNING BLUE SKY
HAVE A GREAT VIEW OF THIS THREE-WIDE
ACTION AT THE 2001 DAYTONA 500.

GIVING FANS A SPARK

IT WOULD BE HARD TO FIND A HELMET FOR THIS
CORPORATE MASCOT, ENTERTAINING FANS BEFORE
THE SAMSUNG/RADIO SHACK 500 AT THE TEXAS
MOTOR SPEEDWAY IN FORT WORTH, TEXAS.
EVERYTHING IS BIGGER IN TEXAS.

CANDY HAS LEGS?

WELL, NO, BUT THIS PHOTO OF A CREW
MEMBER HARD AT WORK UNDER ELLIOTT
SADLER'S M&Ms-SPONSORED CAR SURE
MAKES IT LOOK OTHERWISE.

HAPPY CAMPER

You'd be smiling like Junior Johnson if you had his life, too. One of NASCAR's great all-time personalities, Junior got his start running moonshine, but turned legit and won 50 NASCAR races. Becoming a car owner, his drivers captured six season championships.

MILLION DOLLAR BILL

BILL ELLIOTT GOT THAT NICKNAME FOR PICKING
UP A $1 MILLION BONUS PURSE IN 1985. ALSO
KNOWN AS "AWESOME BILL FROM DAWSONVILLE"
(GEORGIA, THAT IS), HE WAS VOTED "MOST POPULAR
DRIVER" A RECORD 16 TIMES BY NASCAR FANS.

CAN'T DO IT WITHOUT THEM
PREVIOUS SPREAD:
Thanks to growing national interest in stock car racing, NASCAR's attendance has skyrocketed in recent years. In 2003, NASCAR drew more than 6.7 million people to races at two dozen tracks all over the country.

MULTI-TASKING
NASCAR drivers, such as Robby Gordon here during the 2003 Sirius at the Glen At Watkins Glen International in upstate New York, must be skilled on twisting road courses like this one, as well as short tracks and high-banked superspeedways.

CENTER OF ATTENTION

JEFF GORDON FINDS HIMSELF AT THE MIDDLE OF A
MINI-MEDIA CRUSH. NASCAR DRIVERS ARE AMONG
THE MOST ACCESSIBLE IN THE PRO SPORTS WORLD,
KEEPING THEIR FANS UP TO SPEED
ON THE WORLD OF SPEED.

FROM THE GRANDSTAND

For thousands of fans, NASCAR is best
experienced in person as well as on TV.
These fans line the railings at Daytona to aim
their own cameras down at the track.

SLICK TRACK
PREVIOUS SPREAD:
A TRIO OF CARS HEADS OUT OVER A RAIN-SLICKED
ROAD BEFORE A PRACTICE SESSION AT THE 1999
ATLANTA 500 AT THE ATLANTA MOTOR SPEEDWAY
IN HAMPTON, GEORGIA.

FINALLY
AFTER MORE THAN 20 TRIES, DALE EARNHARDT, SR.,
FINALLY CAME OUT ON TOP AT THE DAYTONA 500 IN
1998. FOLLOWING THE RACE, THE PIT CREWS OF
EVERY TEAM LINED PIT ROAD TO CONGRATULATE ONE
OF THE SPORT'S ALL-TIME BEST.

DALE TIMES THREE
DALE EARNHARDT JR. (LEFT) SPENDS SOME TIME
WITH DAD DALE SR. AND DALE JARRETT (RIGHT)
BEFORE 2000 DAYTONA 500. IN 2004, DALE JR.
JOINED THE OTHER DALES AS A WINNER OF
NASCAR'S MOST PRESTIGIOUS RACE.

43 IN '92

RICHARD PETTY, SHOWN HERE IN HIS FAMILIAR
NO. 43 CAR DURING 1992, HIS FINAL RACING
SEASON, IS NASCAR'S ALL-TIME LEADER
IN RACE VICTORIES WITH 200. HIS SEVEN
NASCAR CHAMPIONSHIPS ARE TIED FOR THE
MOST EVER. STILL ACTIVE AS A CAR OWNER,
PETTY IS TRULY "THE KING."

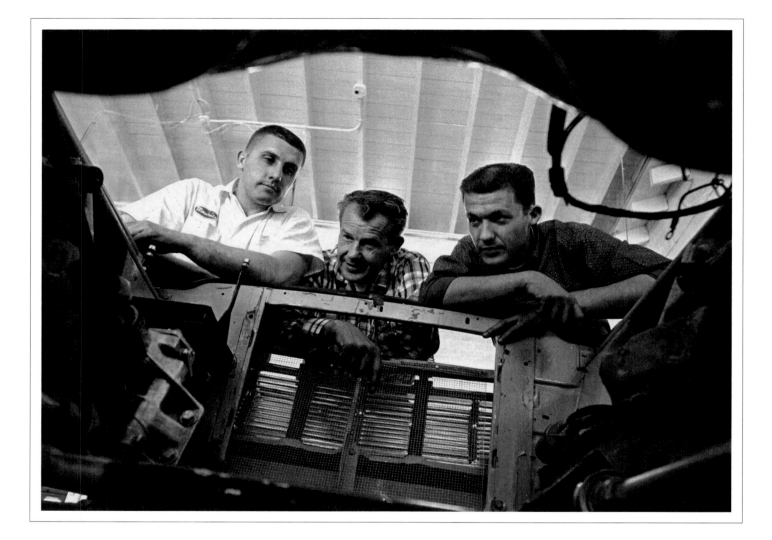

THE FIRST FAMILY

RACING IS ALL IN THE FAMILY FOR THE PETTYS OF
NORTH CAROLINA. LEE (CENTER) WAS THE
PATRIARCH, WINNING 55 NASCAR RACES AND
GUIDING HIS BOYS TO THE TRACK. MAURICE WAS THE
ENGINEER AND RICHARD (RIGHT), WELL, HE TURNED
OUT TO BE A PRETTY GOOD DRIVER, TOO.

BROTHERS IN WHEELS

BOBBY AND TERRY LABONTE ARE ONE OF SEVERAL
PAIRS OF BROTHERS WHO HAVE SHARED THE
NASCAR TRACK. BUT THESE TWO SIBLINGS SHARE
ONE IMPORTANT DISTINCTION: THEY'RE THE ONLY
PAIR OF BROTHERS TO EACH WIN NASCAR TITLES,
TERRY IN 1984 AND 1996 AND BOBBY IN 2000.

NOT TIRED YET
PREVIOUS SPREAD:
NASCAR CREWS CARE FOR THEIR
TIRES WITH CAREFUL PRECISION,
KNOWING THAT CHOOSING THE RIGHT
TIRE CAN LEAD TO VICTORY.

READY WITH THE GAS
GEARED UP WITH FIREPROOF CLOTHING
FROM HEAD TO TOE, THE GAS MAN AND
THE CATCH-CAN MAN FROM JAMIE
MCMURRAY'S TEAM (ABOVE) WAIT AT
TALLADEGA IN 2003.

FOCUS ON THE FUTURE
CREW MEMBERS, LIKE THIS HELMETED
MEMBER OF JEFF GREEN'S TEAM, TAKE
THE FEW QUIET MOMENTS BEFORE A
RACE BEGINS TO GATHER THEIR
THOUGHTS FOR THE ACTION TO COME.

GETTING INTO THEIR WORK
SOMETIMES YOU JUST HAVE TO GET IN THERE AND
GET YOUR HANDS DIRTY, AS THESE CREW MEMBERS
ON (OR SHOULD WE SAY "IN"?) JOHNNY BENSON'S
1996 CAR DEMONSTRATE (ABOVE).

IT TAKES A VILLAGE
WELL, NOT A VILLAGE, BUT A BIG CREW OF EXPERTS.
JEFF GORDON'S CREW SURROUNDS THEIR CAR
BEFORE THE 2003 PENNSYLVANIA 500 AT POCONO
RACEWAY IN LONG POND, PENNSYLVANIA (RIGHT).

SWEET SPRAY OF SUCCESS
PREVIOUS SPREAD:
GREG ZIPADELLI, CREW CHIEF FOR
TONY STEWART'S NO. 20 CAR, ENJOYS
A CHAMPAGNE SPLASH WITH TONY'S
GIRLFRIEND JAIME SHAFFER AFTER
TONY AND GREG'S TEAM WON THE
2002 FORD 400 AT HOMESTEAD-MIAMI.

THE STORM
TODD BODINE'S CREW DEMONSTRATES
THE PRECISE TIMING THAT MAKES
A SUCCESSFUL PIT CREW DURING
THE 1998 COCA-COLA 600 AT
LOWE'S (ABOVE).

THE AFTERMATH
IN THE MAD DASH TO GET EVERYTHING
READY FOR A BIG RACE, A MOMENT
OF CALM MEANS CREW MEMBERS,
LIKE THIS FELLOW FROM MATT
KENSETH'S TEAM (RIGHT), GRAB A
FEW WINKS WHEN THEY CAN.

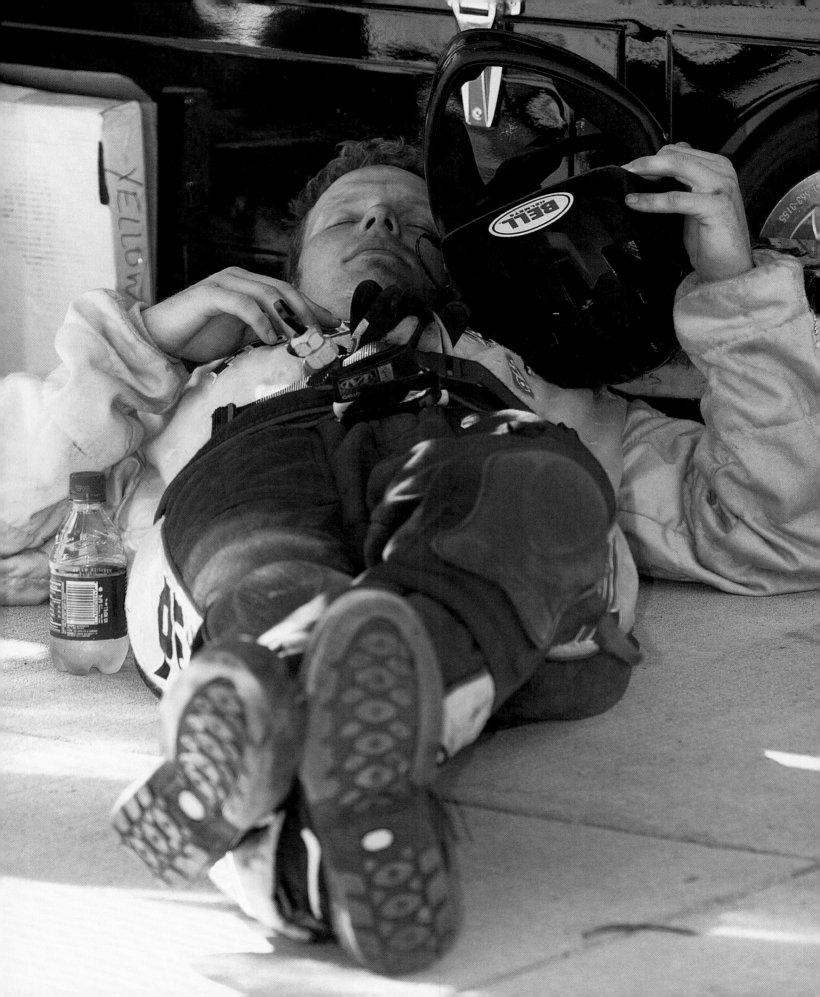

FAST AND FUZZY
PREVIOUS SPREAD:
BOBBY LABONTE LEADS THE PACK DURING THE 1999
DAYTONA 500. JAMIE SQUIRE'S CAMERA HAS FROZEN
THE CARS ON THE TRACK WHILE ALSO CAPTURING
THE SENSE OF SPEED FELT BY FANS.

GETTING AIR
DRIVERS TEST THEIR DRIVING AND FLYING SKILLS ON
THE TIGHT TURNS OF INFINEON RACEWAY IN SONOMA,
CALIFORNIA. HERE (ABOVE), FROM A 1999 RACE,
BOBBY LABONTE CORNERS ON TWO WHEELS AFTER
BUMPING OVER A RETAINER.

THREE WIDE
THE HIGH BANKS AT TALLADEGA SUPERSPEEDWAY
MAKE FOR EXCITING, CLOSE-PACKED ACTION (RIGHT).
IN THE 2000 DIEHARD 500 THERE, EVENTUAL
WINNER JEFF GORDON (BOTTOM LEFT) LEADS THE
WAY THROUGH A TURN.

TRUCKIN'
PREVIOUS SPREAD:
THE NEWEST OF NASCAR'S THREE TOP DIVISIONS,
THE NASCAR CRAFTSMAN TRUCK SERIES PITS
MODIFIED PICKUP TRUCKS IN ACTION ON THE SAME
TRACKS THAT NASCAR NEXTEL CUP AND NASCAR
BUSCH SERIES EVENTS ARE HELD. SHOWN HERE IS
ACTION FROM THE 2002 SEASON.

GATHERING THOUGHTS
HIS EARPLUGS IN AND HIS MIC CORD WAITING TO BE
HOOKED UP, A DRIVER TAKES A MOMENT TO GET
READY BEFORE THE START OF A RACE.

SMILING NOW, BUT . . .
BOBBY LABONTE AND JEFF GORDON ARE ALL LAUGHS
AND SMILES NOW, BUT ONCE THE GREEN FLAG DROPS
IT'LL BE ALL BUSINESS FOR THESE RACIN' PALS.

INTO THE MIST
PREVIOUS SPREAD:
AT THE 2003 SIRIUS AT THE GLEN RACE, THIS LINE
OF CARS HEADING INTO PIT ROAD FOR SERVICE LOOKS
AS IF THEY ARE HEADING INTO A MIRAGE, AS THE
HEAT OFF THE TRACK CREATES SHIMMERING AIR IN
THE DISTANCE.

REAR VIEW MIRROR
IS THIS A SIGN OF HOPE OR A WORD OF WARNING TO
FUTURE NASCAR DRIVERS? MORE AND MORE YOUNG
FANS ARE PICTURING THEMSELVES BEHIND THE
WHEEL SOMEDAY, LIKE THIS FELLOW WATCHING HIS
HEROES AT THE CALIFORNIA 500.

SPLISH, SPLASH

EVEN THE CAR GETS A SORT OF UMBRELLA DURING A
RAIN DELAY AT 2003'S UAW/DAIMLER-CHRYSLER 400
AT LAS VEGAS MOTOR SPEEDWAY, LAS VEGAS,
NEVADA. NASCAR RACES ARE NOT NORMALLY RUN IN
WET CONDITIONS FOR THE SAFETY OF THE DRIVERS.

YOU'VE COME A LONG WAY . . .
FROM CONVERTIBLES ON A TIGHT BEACH COURSE IN
FRONT OF A FEW SPECTATORS (LEFT) TO MODERN
SPEED MACHINES ON HUGE SPEEDWAYS IN FRONT OF
HUNDREDS OF THOUSANDS OF DIEHARD FANS.

FATHER AND SON DAY
IN A SCENE POIGNANT TO ANY NASCAR FAN, DALE EARNHARDT SR. (NO. 3) LEADS DALE EARNHARDT JR. (NO. 8) DURING THE START OF THE 2001 DAYTONA 500.

RICKY IN THE RIVER

RICKY RUDD LOOKS FOR A NEW WAY TO COOL OFF
HIS ENGINE FOLLOWING A SPINOUT TO THE INFIELD
AT LOWE'S MOTOR SPEEDWAY DURING THE 2003
COCA-COLA 600.

BOBBY IN THE SOUP

BOBBY LABONTE WASN'T HURT WHEN HIS RIDE GOT A
LITTLE TOO HOT DURING THE 2003 TROPICANA 400
AT CHICAGOLAND SPEEDWAY IN JOLIET, ILLINOIS,
BUT HIS CAR WAS A LITTLE WORSE
FOR THE WEAR AFTERWARD.

A GREAT PLACE TO RACE
PREVIOUS SPREAD:
A FISH-EYE LENS GIVES A UNIQUE LOOK AT THE TIGHT
TURNS OF THE FAN-FRIENDLY BRISTOL MOTOR
SPEEDWAY IN TENNESSEE. DALE JARRETT'S NO. 88
CAR IS IN THE FOREGROUND OF THIS 2000 PHOTO.

GREEN MEANS GO
HERE'S THE VIEW FROM THE STARTER'S BOOTH AT
PHOENIX (ARIZONA) INTERNATIONAL RACEWAY FOR
THIS WINSTON WEST SERIES EVENT IN 2003.

A FAN CHECKS IN

THIS YOUNG FAN IS EQUIPPED WITH ALL THE GEAR HE
NEEDS TO ENJOY A DAY OF NASCAR RACING AT
INFINEON RACEWAY.

THE GOOD OL' DAYS
JUNIOR JOHNSON'S NO. 55 CAR LEADS THE WAY
AROUND THE TURN IN AN EARLY NASCAR RACE
(ABOVE). THAT'S RIGHT, FANS, THEY'RE RACIN' ON
DIRT, SHORT-TRACK DIRT AT THAT. NONE OF THAT
FANCY ASPHALT STUFF FOR THESE BOYS.

THE FANCY FUTURE
OF COURSE, TODAY'S RACERS DON'T MIND
THE SMOOTH RIDE PROVIDED BY MODERN TRACKS,
AS SHOWN IN THIS ACTION FROM LOWE'S MOTOR
SPEEDWAY DURING 2003 (RIGHT).

MARLIN ON THE MOVE

NASCAR VETERAN STERLING MARLIN IS ONE OF THE MANY DRIVERS FOR WHOM RACING IS AN ART FORM. AT WATKINS GLEN IN 2001, PHOTOGRAPHER BRIAN CLEARY COMBINES MARLIN'S ART WITH HIS OWN TO CREATE A PICTURE OF SPEED IN ACTION.

PRE-RACE PREP

MORE THAN EVER BEFORE, PIT CREW MEMBERS
APPROACH THEIR WORK AS ATHLETES DO, LIFTING
WEIGHTS DURING THE WEEK AND CAREFULLY
STRETCHING OUT BEFORE EACH RACE,
AS THIS MEMBER OF MIKE SKINNER'S CREW
DOES AT DARLINGTON (SOUTH CAROLINA) RACEWAY.

ANOTHER KIND OF STRETCH

WELL, TWO MORE ACTUALLY . . . STRETCHING OUT
OVER THE HOME STRETCH, AN OFFICIAL WAVES THE
YELLOW CAUTION FLAG DURING A 2003 NASCAR
BUSCH SERIES RACE AT TEXAS MOTOR SPEEDWAY.

UNDER THE LIGHTS
PREVIOUS SPREAD:
THIS LIGHT'S-EYE VIEW OF BRISTOL MOTOR
SPEEDWAY CAPTURES THE EXCITEMENT OF NIGHT
RACING, THE TIGHT TURNS, AND THE FULL HOUSE
THAT MAKE THE TENNESSEE TRACK A FAN FAVORITE.

MAN ON BLACK
BEFORE THE 1999 UAW/DAIMLER-CHRYSLER RACE AT
LAS VEGAS, DALE EARNHARDT SR. TAKES A MOMENT
TO RELAX ON SOME TIRES DURING BREAK IN
A PRACTICE SESSION.

THINKING OF A HERO

Fans everywhere were devastated by the
passing in 2001 of Dale Earnhardt Sr.
This young man expressed the feelings of many
with his suddenly poignant jacket.

TWO TONYS

TONY STEWART'S NO. 20 HOME DEPOT CAR IS
REFLECTED IN AN INFIELD PUDDLE DURING THE
2003 POCONO 500.

RAIN DELAY ART

THE CARS OF DALE EARNHARDT JR. AND JEFF
BURTON—AND THEIR REFLECTIONS—FORM A SHINY
TABLEAU IN THE RAIN DURING A STOP DURING THE
2003 TROPICANA 400 AT CHICAGOLAND SPEEDWAY.

TIME TO GET TO WORK

BILL ELLIOTT'S CREW WAITS FOR JUST THE RIGHT
SECOND TO GET OVER THE WALL AND INTO ACTION
(ABOVE). THE PRECISE BALLET OF A PIT STOP BEGINS
ONLY WITH THE DRIVER HITTING HIS MARK EXACTLY.

IN THE PITS AT INDY

JACKED UP ON ONE SIDE, JEREMY MAYFIELD WAITS
FOR HIS PIT CREW TO FINISH CHANGING HIS TIRES SO
HE CAN GET BACK OUT ONTO THE INDIANAPOLIS
(INDIANA) MOTOR SPEEDWAY TRACK DURING THE
2003 BRICKYARD 400 (RIGHT).

FIREBALL IN THE DIRT

GLENN "FIREBALL" ROBERTS WAS AMONG THE TOP
DRIVERS OF NASCAR'S EARLY DAYS. HE ACTUALLY GOT
HIS NICKNAME FROM HIS PITCHING ON THE BASEBALL
FIELD, NOT HIS DRIVING, BUT HIS WHEEL SKILLS WERE
GOOD ENOUGH FOR 32 CAREER WINS.

SOUTHEASTERN FORD DEALE

TESTAMENT TO STEEL

RYAN NEWMAN ESCAPED SERIOUS INJURY FROM
THIS WILD CRASH DURING THE 2003 DAYTONA 500.
TODAY'S NASCAR RIDES ARE DESIGNED TO
WITHSTAND WRECKS THAT IN YEARS PAST MIGHT
HAVE BEEN FAR MORE DANGEROUS.

TEXAS SIZE SPIN OUT

Ryan Newman demonstrates the modern victory
celebration by spinning out on the infield
after his win in the 2003 Samsung/Radio Shack
500 at Texas Motor Speedway.

PIT STOP BALLET
PREVIOUS SPREAD:
AT THE 2002 TROPICANA 400 AT CHICAGOLAND
SPEEDWAY, STERLING MARLIN'S CREW LEAPS INTO
ACTION, THEIR PRECISE CHOREOGRAPHY THE EQUAL
(PLUS HELMETS) OF ANY SEEN ON BROADWAY.

ONE HOT CAR
JOHN ANDRETTI LIGHTS UP THE NIGHT AS A BROKEN
PART OF HIS CAR'S FRAME DRAGS ON THE TRACK,
SHOOTING UP SPARKS ON HIS WAY
TO THE PITS FOR REPAIR.

ALL TOGETHER NOW

DAVE BLANEY GETS A LITTLE HELP FROM HIS
FRIENDS ON HIS WAY TO THE START LINE AT THE
2003 AARONS 499 AT TALLADEGA.

BEFORE AND AFTER
PIT ROAD IS A WHIRLING MASS OF COLOR, ACTION,
AND EQUIPMENT DURING THE 1999 UAW/DAIMLER-
CHRYSLER RACE AT LAS VEGAS (LEFT). BUT MOMENTS
LATER (ABOVE) ALL THAT IS LEFT IS SKID MARKS.

KEEP ON TRUCKIN'

ANOTHER KIND OF WHEELMAN IS NEARLY AS VITAL
TO A NASCAR TEAM AS THE DRIVER. THAT'S THE
PERSON WHO STEERS ONE OF THESE 18-WHEELERS
FROM TRACK TO TRACK EACH WEEK, EACH TRUCK
FILLED WITH CARS, ENGINES, AND OTHER GEAR.

RACING RAINBOW
A LINE OF NASCAR'S BEST MAKES A COLORFUL
ARRAY JUST BEFORE THE START OF THE 2003
VIRGINIA 500 AT MARTINSVILLE SPEEDWAY.

PREMIUM OR REGULAR?

Just like you and the family car, NASCAR's best have to make a stop at the old fillin' station every once in a while. Here a trio of cars gasses up during practice at Talladega in 2003.

THREE WIDE THEN

Slam-bang, close-quarters racin' from the
early 1950s, as Marshall Teague in the No. 6
Hudson Hornet slides by on the inside while
two of his opponents tangle on the upside.

PACK RACING

No. 12 Joe Weatherly holds the high line in
the 1959 Daytona Firecracker 250.
No. 47 Jack Smith has the inside track in his
Thunderbird. Weatherly would later become
the 1962 and 1963 NASCAR champ.

RECORD-SETTING MARGIN

PREVIOUS SPREAD:

PHOTOGRAPHER BRIAN CLEARY CAPTURED THIS
PHOTO-FINISH ACTION AT DARLINGTON IN 2003.
RICKY CRAVEN (32) WON THE RACE BY .002 SECONDS
OVER KURT BUSCH IN THE CLOSEST FINISH IN
NASCAR HISTORY.

READY TO RACE (ALMOST)

THE CAR IS READY, THE CREW IS PUMPED, NOW IT'S
TIME TO TAKE A MOMENT AND PAUSE DURING THE
PLAYING OF THE NATIONAL ANTHEM BEFORE THE
BEGINNING OF THE 2003 COCA-COLA 600
AT LOWE'S MOTOR SPEEDWAY.

READY TO PARTY

TERRY LABONTE'S CREW JUMPS FOR JOY AS THEIR
DRIVER WINS THE 2003 SOUTHERN 500 AT
DARLINGTON. GOT MILK?, THEIR SUITS ASK . . .
SURE, GOT A TRIP TO VICTORY LANE, TOO!

GOTTA KISS THE BRICKS

IN 2000, BOBBY LABONTE (ABOVE RIGHT) AND CREW
CHIEF JIMMY MAKAR CONTINUED A NASCAR TRADITION
UNLIKE NO OTHER (THANK GOODNESS) BY KISSING THE
HISTORIC STRIP OF BRICK AT THE INDIANAPOLIS MOTOR
SPEEDWAY AFTER WINNING THE BRICKYARD 400.

REACH FOR THE SKY

KEVIN HARVICK'S LIPS, MEANWHILE, WILL REMAIN
TEMPORARILY BRICK-DUST-FREE AFTER HE CLIMBS
DOWN TO ACCEPT CONGRATULATIONS FOR WINNING
THE 2003 BRICKYARD 400 AT INDIANAPOLIS (RIGHT).

GEOMETRY MEETS SPEED

PREVIOUS SPREAD:
THIS OVERHEAD VIEW OF INFINEON SPEEDWAY IN
NORTHERN CALIFORNIA SHOWS THE DISTINCTIVE
SHORT, TIGHT TURNS OF A ROAD COURSE.
INFINEON IS ONE OF TWO THAT REGULARLY PLAY
HOST TO NEXTEL CUP EVENTS.

REPEATING PETTYS

NASCAR DRIVERS WOULD CALL THIS A NIGHTMARE,
NINE RICHARD PETTYS! ONE WAS GOOD ENOUGH
TO WIN MORE RACES THAN ANY OTHER DRIVER
IN NASCAR HISTORY.

JACKPOT!

MATT KENSETH POSES WITH SOME OTHER LOCAL
HEROES AFTER WINNING THE 2003
UAW-DAIMLERCHRYSLER 400 AT,
OBVIOUSLY, LAS VEGAS.

FACE OF A WINNER

DALE JARRETT (LEFT) HAS BEEN ONE OF NASCAR'S
ELITE DRIVERS FOR NEARLY TWO DECADES. FROM 1996
TO 2001, HE FINISHED IN THE TOP FIVE EVERY YEAR,
INCLUDING THE NO. 1 SPOT IN 1999. HE HAD AT LEAST
ONE WIN EACH YEAR FROM 1993 THROUGH 2003,
INCLUDING THE 2003 SUBWAY 400 (ABOVE)
AT NORTH CAROLINA SPEEDWAY IN ROCKINGHAM,
NORTH CAROLINA.

A REAL GOODY

WINNING A RACE IS ONE THING, BUT A HUG FROM
YOUR DAUGHTER IS MUCH, MUCH BETTER.
AT THE GOODY'S DASH RACE AT DAYTONA IN 2003,
ROBERT HUFFMAN GOT BOTH.

DIFFERENT KINDS OF GOODIES

You'd think after winning the 2003 EA Sports
500 at Talladega, Dale Earnhardt Jr. could
have found someone else to sweep up . . .
then again, he did earn all that money.

TAKEOFF!

FOLLOWING A PRERACE VISIT BY PRESIDENT GEORGE W. BUSH TO THE 2004 DAYTONA 500, AIR FORCE ONE (ABOVE) ROSE MAJESTICALLY BEHIND THE GRANDSTANDS, GIVING RACE FANS A CLOSE-UP VIEW OF SOMETHING ELSE GOING REALLY, REALLY FAST.

SPLASHDOWN!

BOBBY LABONTE (RIGHT) NEEDS A TOWEL BEFORE HE CAN PICK UP HIS VICTORY CHECK AS HIS CREW MAKES LIKE A FOOTBALL TEAM AND GREETS HIM WITH A GATORADE SHOWER FOLLOWING HIS WIN IN THE 2003 ATLANTA 500.

GETTING IN

NASCAR VEHICLES DON'T HAVE DOORS, SO WHEN
SOMEONE HAS TO GET INSIDE (IN THIS CASE A PIT
CREW MEMBER SERVICING KURT BUSCH'S CAR IN
1999 AT TALLADEGA) HEADING IN THROUGH THE
WINDOW IS THE ONLY OPTION.

GETTING OUT

MICHAEL WALTRIP MAKES LIKE A JACK-IN-THE-BOX,
SHOWING OFF BOTH HIS NEW ROOF ACCESS PANEL
AND HIS CELEBRATION STYLE AS HIS CREW RACES
OVER TO GREET HIM AFTER HIS WIN IN THE
2003 DAYTONA 500.

BACK IN THE DAY
PREVIOUS SPREAD:
BEFORE HE BECAME THE "MAN IN BLACK," DALE EARNHARDT SR. WAS THE MAN IN THE WRANGLER JEANS. HERE HE GIVES A WAVE AS HE CROSSES UNDER THE CHECKERED FLAG AT DARLINGTON IN THE 1986 TRANS SOUTH 500.

INDIANA MONKEYS
KEVIN HARVICK'S CREW SCAMPERED UP THE TRACKSIDE FENCE WITH GLEE AFTER THEIR MAN WON THE 2003 BRICKYARD 400 AT THE VENERABLE INDIANAPOLIS MOTOR SPEEDWAY.

OTHER SIDE OF THE FENCE

JUST INCHES FROM THEIR HEROES, FANS LINE THE
PIT AREA FENCE DURING PRACTICE AT THE
PENNSYLVANIA 500 AT POCONO RACEWAY FOR SOME
AUTOGRAPHS, A FEW HANDSHAKES,
AND SOME QUICK SNAPSHOTS.

BACK HOME IN INDIANA

JEFF GORDON (LEFT) GREW UP IN INDIANA, IN THE SHADOW OF THE INDIANAPOLIS MOTOR SPEEDWAY. THAT HISTORY MADE THIS 1998 BRICKYARD 400 VICTORY CELEBRATION EVEN SWEETER.

TEXAS TWO STEP

AT THE NASCAR CRAFTSMAN TRUCK SERIES O'REILLY 400 RACE IN 2003 AT TEXAS MOTOR SPEEDWAY, BRENDAN GAUGHAN (ABOVE) KEPT ON TRUCKIN' INTO VICTORY LANE WHERE THE BED OF HIS PICKUP MADE A DANDY CELEBRATION PLATFORM.

EAT HIS DUST!
CALE YARBOROUGH WAS ONE OF **NASCAR**'S ALL-TIME
LEGENDS, A DRIVER WHO PUT IN A LOT OF MILES
BEFORE REALIZING HIS POTENTIAL TO BE THE BEST.
CALE WON THREE STRAIGHT **NASCAR** CROWNS
(1976–78) AND FINISHED SECOND OVERALL
THREE TIMES AS WELL.

MY MAN THE WINNER

CALE YARBOROUGH'S 83 LIFETIME VICTORIES IN
NASCAR PLACE HIM AMONG THE ALL-TIME LEADERS.
ONE OF THOSE WINS CAME HERE AT THE 1983
COCA-COLA 600 HELD IN ATLANTA, WHERE HE
WAS GREETED BY HIS WIFE, BETTY JO.

DESERT VIEW

AMID THE ROCKS, SAND, AND CACTUS OVERLOOKING
PHOENIX INTERNATIONAL RACEWAY ARE A GATHERING
OF DIEHARD FANS WHO HAVE FOUND A UNIQUE VIEW
OF THE TRACK.

AGONY AND . . .
WINNERS CRY, TOO. 2001 DAYTONA 500
WINNER MICHAEL WALTRIP (ABOVE) REACTS
AFTER HE HEARS THAT DALE EARNHARDT SR.
DIED DURING A CRASH JUST BEFORE THE END
OF WALTRIP'S VICTORY.

. . . ECSTASY
CONFETTI FLIES IN VICTORY LANE AS
KURT BUSCH (RIGHT) LEAPS FROM HIS CAR
INTO THE WAITING ARMS OF HIS CREW. BUSCH
HAD JUST WON THE 2002 FORD 400 AT
HOMESTEAD IN MIAMI.

FIRST HE SPINS . . .

MATT KENSETH DIDN'T WIN THIS RACE AT THE NORTH
CAROLINA SPEEDWAY IN 2003, BUT HE GOT TO DO A
POST-RACE VICTORY SPINOUT. FOR THE REASON WHY,
LOOK TO THE RIGHT.

. . . THEN THEY WIN

MATT'S FOURTH-PLACE FINISH AT THAT NORTH
CAROLINA RACE WAS ENOUGH TO CLINCH THE 2003
NASCAR WINSTON CUP SERIES CHAMPIONSHIP FOR
THE YOUNG DRIVER, AND HIS PIT CREW (ABOVE)
BEGAN THE CELEBRATION.

DASH AT DUSK

THE SUN IS GOING DOWN, BUT THE ACTION IS HEATING UP AT DAYTONA INTERNATIONAL SPEEDWAY DURING THE 2000 PEPSI 400.

JUMPIN' FOR JOY

AFTER ROARING TO VICTORY IN ATLANTA IN 1997,
JEFF GORDON LEAPED FOR JOY. THE WIN GAVE THE
YOUNG DRIVER HIS SECOND NASCAR WINSTON CUP
SERIES CHAMPIONSHIP.

FOUR FOR 24

WITH FOUR NASCAR WINSTON CUP SERIES
CHAMPIONSHIPS, JEFF GORDON, SHOWN HERE IN
ACTION FROM 2003, TRAILS ONLY RICHARD PETTY
AND DALE EARNHARDT JR.'S SEVEN TITLES EACH ON
THE LIST OF ALL-TIME CHAMPS.

WORK NEVER SLEEPS
PREVIOUS SPREAD:
SUNSET JUST MEANS THE END OF A DAY, NOT THE END OF THE WORK FOR THESE *NASCAR* CREWS AT PHOENIX IN 2003. THEY'LL WORK ALL NIGHT IF NECESSARY TO PREPARE FOR THE RACE AHEAD.

FUTURE CHAMP?
THE FLAT BLEACHERS AT PHOENIX INTERNATIONAL RACEWAY BEFORE A NASCAR BUSCH SERIES RACE MAKE A PERFECT TRACK FOR THIS YOUNG FAN TO TEST THE SPEED OF HIS TOY CAR. MAYBE WE'LL SEE HIM IN THE **2024** EDITION OF *NASCAR BEST SHOTS*.